PHILOSOPHY:
A CHRISTIAN PERSPECTIVE

AN INTRODUCTORY ESSAY

ARTHUR F. HOLMES

*INTER-VARSITY PRESS
DOWNERS GROVE, ILLINOIS 60515*

Third printing, October 1977

InterVarsity Press is the book
publishing division of Inter-Varsity
Christian Fellowship, a student
movement active on campus at hundreds
of universities, colleges and
schools of nursing. For information
about local and regional activities,
write IVCF, 233 Langdon St.,
Madison, WI 53703.

Distributed in Canada through InterVarsity
Press, 745 Mount Pleasant Rd.,
Toronto, M4S 2N5.

ISBN 0-87784-424-0

Printed in the United
States of America

CONTENTS

Introduction

Twentieth-century Christianity faces a pagan world. Once Christian beliefs and values gave direction to society and meaning to art and science and all of life, but today not only is the truth of these beliefs denied but their meaningfulness also is forgotten and new moralities have arisen. The vacuum is being filled by Eastern religions, by a new wave of romanticism and pragmatism, by existentialist philosophies and, of course, by various kinds of Marxism. Rapprochements from time to time appear between Christianity and Marxism, Christianity and existentialism, Christianity and positivism and so forth, posing again in our day the ageless problem of how we can relate faith to reason, and more particularly Christianity to philosophy.

First-century Christianity itself was born into a philosophically minded pagan culture. Alexander the Great had sought to impose Greek thought patterns on the eastern Mediterranean world; Antiochus Epiphanes attempted to do the same with the Jews; and Rome triumphed in the East only to be consumed by the octopus-like tentacles of Hellenism. Consequently, early Christianity confronted a philosophically minded Greco-Roman world and was nurtured by a Judaism that had its

Hellenists as well as its culturally isolationist Pharisees. From its earliest years, therefore, the church was compelled to come to grips with questions about the relationship of Christianity to philosophy.

The church's perennial interest in this problem has taken a variety of forms. Some individuals and groups, suspicious either of philosophic infiltration into theology or of the soul-callousing effect of intellectualism, repudiated philosophy as intrinsically unchristian. Others, impressed by parallels between the statements of certain philosophers and those of the Jewish and Christian Scriptures, uncritically embraced as essentially Christian not only the philosophic enterprise but also particular philosophic viewpoints and conclusions. Others again, recognizing the legitimacy of what philosophers try to do but not of everything they have done, attempted to work out syntheses that would preserve the unique contributions of biblical Christianity. Others again conceived of a distinctively Christian philosophy.

The twentieth-century Christian who examines the record cannot avoid the conclusion that the main stream of historic orthodoxy has followed neither of the first two avenues; it has been neither obscurantist nor rationalist. He is compelled to develop for himself a working relationship between Christianity and philosophy that will discredit neither Christianity nor philosophy. Basic to this task is an understanding of the nature of the two enterprises involved. All too often the repudiation of philosophy, whether by significant writers or by popular Christian sentiment, stems from a failure to appreciate what philosophers are actually trying to do. With similar frequency a rejection or compromise of the faith stems from a failure to appreciate the full intent and broad relevance of Christianity.

The present book, then, is an attempt to introduce and in a limited way to explore the relation of reason and revelation by trying to understand the nature of philosophy and of Christianity respectively. In its brief compass it can be suggestive, but neither exhaustive nor conclusive.

CHAPTER 1

What Is Philosophy?

Pythagoras was supposedly the first to call himself a *philosopher*. In coining this term, he intended to use it literally: The philosopher is a "lover of wisdom." Two implications have remained true of subsequent philosophy. First, it involves one in a persistent and resolute quest that refuses to be satisfied with glib answers and over-simplified solutions. It is a logically disciplined and self-critical inquiry. Second, its goal of wisdom, *sophia*, brooks neither idle curiosity nor a coldly impersonal amassing of miscellaneous information. Rather, philosophy addresses questions that are basic to man's understanding of himself, his world and his God, that is, questions that are basic to life itself.

The popular concept of a "philosophy of life" or a "world view" makes sense in this context. It suggests a reflective outlook on life as a whole which gives meaning to the parts, ties our beliefs and values together, and provides a sense of direction amid life's innumerable paths. We speak of taking reverses or bad news "philosophically," that is to say, with a patience born of mature reflection on the basic issues of life.

These, however, are popular rather than technical usages. They illustrate the combination of thoughtful reflection and practical concern, but they are still more representative of the homespun ideas of the man-in-the-street than of the interests and rigor of the professional philosopher. Philosophy today is far more than philosophy of life, and often it is not that at all. Like other inquiries it has achieved a degree of technicality that can bewilder the novice.

Philosophy, moreover, must be distinguished from the sciences and from theology and the arts. The ancients included all the sciences within the general pale of philosophy, and less than a century ago the natural sciences were still called "natural philosophy." We separate them. Yet today's departmentalizing of philosophy and the sciences does not mean that philosophers are unconcerned with the subject matter of other disciplines. They are concerned with it at a different level, not at a factual or experimental level, but at the foundational level of questions about the logic of scientific explanation and the presuppositions of science. And they work in a different way, not by using empirical or statistical methods, but with greater abstraction from the world of particulars and with closer attention to logical argument and the meaning of language.

Some early Christian writers, adopting the ancient use of "philosophy," called Christianity a philosophy. Yet while Christian theology doubtless had philosophical consequences and makes philosophical assumptions, it is more the particular science that studies the teachings of the Christian religion than it is a logical examination of the basic questions which religion in general poses about the existence of God or the logical justification of belief.

Nor is philosophy a creative art to shape the sensory and imaginative possibilities that a world of variegated particulars holds. Yet it is still interested in basic questions which art poses about aesthetic experience, the meaning of symbols, the universal bases of art criticism, and so forth. In fact, philosophical questions arise in every area of life and thought simply because they are basic to everything.

The Nature of Philosophy

Philosophy may be identified, then, by the foundational questions that comprise its subject matter and by its theoretical objectives and logical methods. Aristotle observed that philosophy begins with wonder, with a natural desire to know that does not stop when all the available information is in. It concerns itself with the "first principles" of all the arts and sciences, principles which other disciplines presuppose but which only philosophy examines systematically. Aristotle had in mind such concepts as "substance," "cause," "change" and "time," and such in ethics as "the good" and "justice." Men seek to know what the good life really is and why, and how it may be achieved; what essentially different kinds of substance may be distinguished and whether a purpose pervades all that nature does as well as man.

I call these the "foundational questions" which arise in other disciplines but which philosophy, not science or art, explores. They include (1) questions about knowledge and truth and the justification of belief (epistemology), (2) questions about the essential nature of man, nature and God (metaphysics), (3) questions about the basis of moral values (ethics), (4) questions about aesthetic values, (5) questions about the bases and purposes of organized society (social and political philosophy), and so forth.

But philosophy includes more than foundational questions. It also involves intellectual objectives and the abstract reasoning that distinguishes philosophical methods from the experimental and statistical methods of the sciences and from the artistic creation of new experiences, new forms and new symbols. The philosopher has generally pursued one or both of two objectives. These are, first, a *systematic* understanding of the whole range of philosophical questions and concepts and, second, *clarity* of understanding. In both cases the objective is theoretical (to understand) rather than pragmatic, despite the innumerable practical applications philosophy actually has.

First, the quest for systematic understanding puts philosophy in touch with world views, and for this reason it is the aspect of philosophy most involved with Christianity. It attempts to put all our basic philosophical concepts together into a carefully developed, coherent explanation of the nature of God, man and the universe, the nature of our knowledge of them, and the bearing of all this on our values. Comparatively few philosophers have succeeded in working out enduring systems. The names of Aristotle and Hegel stand as two of the greatest by virtue of their encyclopedic scope and overall vision.

The idea of a philosophical system raises problems which have not escaped the penetrating scrutiny of the less venturesome. The scope of human knowledge is at best limited, and even the vast mass of scientific insight accumulated since the Renaissance seems likely to be but a tiny glimpse of otherwise unimagined vistas. Social ideologies and scientific hypotheses alike undergo change; a man's understanding is inevitably relative to his particular position in space and time; it is open to debate whether man will ever apprehend more than passing phenomena that deceptively shadow unknowable realities. Is it any wonder, it is argued, that world views and philosophical systems come and go with their respective cultures, reflecting as they must a changing *Zeitgeist*, the ever shifting spirit of the age? A truly comprehensive and final system presupposes that we see the *whole* of life steadily and unchangeably. It presupposes the humanly impossible—the viewpoints and abilities of deity.

Inevitably, therefore, the systematic philosopher cannot claim to have developed a final and exhaustive position. But he can lay claim to the quest for a system that builds upon lessons from the past and upon present intimations of the future. He makes a persistent *attempt* to see life as totally and as steadily as is humanly possible, an attempt that admits to fallible interpretations and unsolved problems, yet strives constantly for the scope and self-consistency and coherence which are hallmarks of truth.

Even this fails to satisfy modern objectors. What is known must be intelligible and so, some have said, it must be empirically verifiable—or at least falsifiable. Moreover, is human language adequate to the task? How can words capture and convey the unity and diversity of those multidimensioned realities that lie around man and beyond? How can we talk of God and the soul? Perhaps we must forego the right to say we *know* anything which evades empirical examination or logical analysis. The quest for a philosophical or even a religious world view today supposes that logically prior questions such as these have been satisfactorily answered. It is little wonder that, in most philosophical circles, they dominate the scene and philosophy's second objective has risen to the fore.

Second, the quest for clarity of understanding is evident in much of contemporary English-speaking philosophy. Analytic philosophy is an attempt to clarify concepts and explore their logical relations. While it is detailed work and often seems to focus on piecemeal topics, it still addresses what is foundational to our knowledge or values.

This quest for clarity of understanding is by no means an innovation of twentieth-century analysts. While it is true that the contemporary mind has reemphasized problems of meaning, to some extent it has been a perennial concern of philosophers. Socrates was a classical example; with his renowned dialectical method he sought for unambiguous expression based on a clear understanding of questions and concepts, combined with logical consistency and cogency of argument. The Socratic dialogues are masterpieces of philosophical analysis in the quest for meaning and understanding.

By the same token it is significant that Socrates stimulated the more systematic genius of Plato and Aristotle. The clarification of individual questions introduced still other questions, and these in turn raised issues of a more general and inclusive nature. Analysis became the prelude to system-building. So it has been since. Scholastic analyses of questions regarding God and man, and nature and grace, produced the neo-Aristotelian system of Thomas Aquinas. Enlightenment analyses of the problem of knowledge, stimulated by the growth of physical sciences, generated the philosophies of the nineteenth century. And the work of recent analysts like Wittgenstein has made immense contributions on classic issues of importance to systematic thought.

The quests for clarity and consistency, then, go hand in hand. Consistency and coherence are logical desiderata in a philosophical system, and clarity is the rational desideratum of the analytic quest for understanding. Other requirements of an empirical or even a cultural nature may indeed be involved, but these at least are indispensable.

Philosophy desires clarity, consistency and coherence. Its quest is for a both lucid and systematic understanding of foundational matters. Deliberately or unintentionally obscured notions are as objectionable as self-contradictions. For this reason philosophy is a legitimate human enterprise: Its objectives are essentially those of all rational beings.

It should be recognized, however, that philosophy remains a quest. As long as man's insight is finite, elements of mystery are liable to shroud his otherwise clear understanding. He may probe the reasons for what he observes and analyze concepts and language, but he does so in the *quest* for a degree of clarity that for the present remains elusive. In addition, as long as the scope of man's knowledge is limited, and as long as his systematic reasoning must employ guiding hypotheses and basic presuppositions which admit of no demonstrative certainty, the possibility of error threatens an otherwise consistent position. He may include a greater scope of learning, he may reassess his presuppositions and check his logic, but he does so still in the *quest* for the kind of a system that for the present eludes him. Philosophy is a quest with which dogmatism and obscurantism are equally incompatible.

The Function of Philosophy

The philosophical quest may have intrinsic merit as a satisfying theoretical inquiry, but does it serve any useful purpose in society? To the man-in-the-street, and for the Christian seeking to develop a working relationship to philosophy, the question is crucial. A legitimate yet irrelevant enterprise attracts little interest.

Philosophy is but one cultural activity. Culture as a whole is the developed pattern of human life as it centers around certain key beliefs and values. Philosophy seeks to clarify those beliefs and values, to explore their theoretical bases and to develop a systematic understanding of things. It is culture becoming self-critical and systematically reflective. It is a process of intellectual maturation analogous to that of individuals. The child who cries for the moon wants the yellow ball he sees on the roof of the house next door. The adolescent laughs at his little brother, but finds in the full moon a stimulus to romance and an occasion for fun. The adult, however, sees an object of aesthetic enjoyment or scientific investigation. Intellectual maturation, whether in the individual or in the group, involves a refining of ideas, a re-expression of ideals, a careful sifting of naive notions. Childhood assumptions give way to adolescent attitudes, and these in turn develop into adult viewpoints.

In a maturating culture philosophy provides an intellectual conscience to probe existing thought-patterns, to push thought beyond what is historically or culturally relative, and to argue for what is universally true. It can develop an overall world view as a guide in the processes and conflicts of history. The German philosopher Hegel once said that the nation without a metaphysic is like a temple without a holy of holies. We may add that a nation whose values are not subjected to philosophical scrutiny is like a temple without foundations. Both functions are important.

Socrates exemplifies the first function of philosophy, that of an intellectual conscience for society. Disgusted by political intrigue, concerned about moral relativism, alarmed at signs of cultural disintegration, he sought to expose underlying confusions of mind, to force the development of clear ideas, to encourage the pursuit of true values. In rejecting Socrates, Athens repressed its intellectual conscience. Subsequent philosophers have to various extents served the same function. Philosophical criticism compelled the early church to clarify its understanding of the Trinity. Philosophical insistence on a clear understanding of man forced the development of Renaissance political theories which molded democratic ideals. Careful analysis is needed today of the assumptions both mysticism and pragmatism make about the nature of man, and we need to scrutinize the methods and concepts of contemporary behaviorism. Intellectual confusion is a hazard to the whole of human society, a hazard against which the quest for clear understanding stands guard.

The philosopher-king of Plato's *Republic* illustrates the second cultural function of philosophy, the development of a guiding world view. Plato supposes that the reflective individual, who has gained for himself a clear understanding of true values, will have gained a proper perspective on the down-to-earth issues of daily life. He will approach decisions neither emotively nor with a partisan spirit, but in the light of his overall view of man and his place in the universe. His world view will enable him to rule well.

This ideal admittedly did not prove too practicable. A local situation with its political intrigue and corruption paid scanty respect to Plato's lofty idealism. Yet he recognized that a developed philosophy is an indispensable guide not only for the individual but also for society. It is philosophy which develops the world views that religion and culture propose. In content and acceptability they vary. Marx and Nietzsche, Dewey and Hegel, Locke and

Rousseau, Augustine and Aquinas, Sartre and Marcuse, each has made history by developing an ideology to guide society.

Ours is a pluralistic society. Not one but a variety of world views have been philosophically developed in the West, and the religious and ethical and political ideas and values which once shaped Western civilization no longer rule. The established philosophic traditions have broken down, but the analysis of ideas and the conflict of world views continue in philosophy and elsewhere.

Philosophy is therefore a momentous undertaking that cannot be ignored and must not be underestimated. Its twofold quest endows it with a twofold cultural mission. The relation of revelation to reason must be considered in this context. Christians face a pagan culture in which varied philosophic forces are at work. Christianity's relationship to philosophy will accordingly depend at least in part on Christianity's relationship to human culture.

CHAPTER 2

What Is Christianity?

The Christian message begins with an all-important diagnosis of the nature and need of man. It is addressed to man as a responsible agent who thinks and acts and lives before God, his creator. Man is both a rational being and a moral agent, and so the Christian message assumes he is capable both of understanding the ideas it proclaims and of undertaking responsible moral action. As a responsible and rational agent man stands before God in the image of God and is unique in the earthly creation. He alone is equipped for the interpersonal relations that produce human culture, and for a personal knowledge of and fellowship with God. This image of God in man is marred by sin: His understanding is obscured, his morality debased, his relationships broken. As a result the individual, the group, and their cultural achievements all suffer.

Christianity claims that God reconciles sinful men to himself and so to one another. To that end he enlightens the sinner's understanding by an historical process of revelation climaxing in the incarnation of Jesus Christ, and he remedies moral failure through the personal redemption provided by the incarnate Christ. Because of the impact of God's revelation and redemption on their thinking and living, Christians have had, as we shall observe, a distinctive impact upon the culture of their day. Christianity may therefore be defined as that religion of revelation and redemption which centers in the divine person and historic work of Jesus Christ who reconciles men to God and to one another.

This definition requires further explication. We shall first explore the genus—it is a religion—and then the differentia—revelation and redemption centering in Jesus Christ.

Christianity as a Religion

Philosophy is a cultural activity, but that is hardly true of religion. Its function, its goals and its methods are different, for it stands at the root of everything.

Philosophy is a theoretical inquiry into foundational questions that underlie every area of life and thought. Religion too touches everything, but in a different way. Man's experience with God and his faith in God give him an overall perspective and an ultimate hope that can transform his approach to life and thought. This claim itself poses philosophical questions about the existence of God and the truth-claims of religion, for example, so that the two activities intersect. But the religious function of our beliefs and values is markedly different from their philosophical interest. Religion creates ultimate loyalties, originates our most basic beliefs and values, and transmits and preserves them. Religious experience, both corporate and individual, reinforces beliefs and commitments, and provides a dynamic which can integrate personalities and even unify culture. By suggesting that man's *raison d'être* lies outside himself, it points to values that transcend the changing moods and scenes of the present struggle. In these ways it is not just another cultural activity of an optional sort, nor is it a theoretical activity like philosophy, but it motivates and informs all human activities with its beliefs and values.

Generalizations such as these need to be noted, for while Christianity may indeed be unique among religions, it is still a religion, and as such it is concerned with the ideas and values around which a culture is structured and a philosophy developed. Christianity points men to "the good life," enjoyed both here and hereafter through the knowledge of God. "What is the chief end of man?" asks the Westminster Shorter Catechism. It is "to glorify God and enjoy him forever." Christian experience, both corporate and individual, reinforces this belief and renews one's commitment to its various implications. It provides something of the dynamic which integrates the believer's life and unifies the Christian community. In countries which have most felt the impact of the Judeo-Christian tradition, Christians have played their part in the structuring of culture. As members of society they inevitably helped build the culture. As Christians they inevitably built into it some of the ideas and values rooted in their knowledge of God. Clement and Augustine, Luther and Calvin, Wesley and Wilberforce all played their part. Directly or indirectly they and others had a hand, therefore, in the development of the philosophies of their day and ours.

The Differentia of Christianity

Christianity is a revealed religion; that is to say, it is the product, not of man's ordinary insights into his relationship to God—what we speak of as natural religion—but of God's special revelation of himself. The Old Testament records God's self-manifestation in the history of Israel and the experience of believers, as well as in the utterances of his prophets. The New Testament records God's activity in the development of the early church, its doctrine and its conduct. But the knowledge of God provided and attested by the biblical record is most dramatically presented in Jesus Christ. The entire Bible makes it clear that God's supreme self-revelation occurred in the person and work of his incarnate Son. The Christian revelation centers in the One who claimed, "He who has seen me has seen the Father."

From its earliest days the church has regarded Scripture as its final and sufficient rule of faith and practice. Biblical teachings about God and man, sin and grace, personal and social ethics have given direction to believers' lives and thought, and so guided their theology and philosophy. The Christian revelation is intended to lead man to know God in terms of the truth he learns from Scripture. It is transmitted to man by the vehicle of human language, in a body of literature inspired by the Holy Spirit. For this reason the biblical scholar engages in textual criticism in order to ensure an accurate text; he engages in grammatical and historical exegesis in order to ascertain the intent of the writer's statements; he enters upon every literary science that aids clear and correct understanding of divine revelation.

One caution is necessary at this point. The revelation which brings men to a knowledge of God is not exclusively objective. John Calvin spoke of the inner testimony of the Holy Spirit; Scripture insists that spiritual truths only become personally relevant when impressed upon the mind by God's Spirit. The seed must germinate and take root if it is to produce fruit. But the necessity of a subjective work of God denies neither the objectivity of the truth nor the demand for a careful, rational study of Scripture. It means, rather, that the Holy Spirit operates in conjunction with normal mental processes so as to make the truth meaningful to the individual. In all his works God employs the natural processes he has ordained.

To know and love God is man's highest good. Man is kept from these not only by his ignorance, willful or otherwise, but also by his sin. His moral condition confuses his understanding and hampers both faith and fellowship. He needs not only the revelation but also the redemption provided by the divine person and historic work of Jesus Christ, if he is to be reconciled to God.

Redemption, too, has both objective and subjective sides. The former is seen in the historical work of the Savior in his life on earth, his crucifixion and his resurrection. The latter is seen in the subjective work of the Holy Spirit in transforming the believer—that which theology speaks of as regeneration and sanctification. One may know about God through revelation, but one may only gain a saving knowledge and enter into personal fellowship with God on the basis of redemption and its transforming effect on the moral life and spiritual outlook. The effect is pervasive. Reconciliation to God brings reconciliation to others, so that our attitudes to nature and society, to intellectual and emotional involvements, to the state and the family, are all involved. The Christian brings Christian ideas and values to his culture. He brings the potential for a Christian world view.

The Truth-Claims of Christianity

Christianity claims to be true. Its truth-claims extend to all that the Bible teaches, whether concerning God and his mighty acts in history, or concerning man and his destiny. Here Christianity and philosophy intersect, for both are concerned with truth—the one to proclaim and practice it, and the other to understand it and to examine logically the truth claims that arise.

The claim to truth arouses objections. What have metaphysics, history and miracles to do with Christianity? It has become customary to separate history from faith—to regard truth as changing and relative, or else to lose it in the subjective intensity of an existential experience. In any case Christianity is either compromised by or divorced from the "truth" in other cultural areas—history, science or philosophy.

Three observations seem pertinent to establishing a relationship between Christianity and philosophy that will compromise neither Christianity nor philosophy. First, it should be observed at this stage that because of inevitable limitations on human knowledge, there will remain areas of problem and mystery. We shall return to this point in the final chapter. Second, the doctrine of twofold truth in either its old or its new forms is not ultimately satisfying to either the philosopher or the theologian. It has been the position of historic Christianity that truth is one. What is historically untrue or logically contradictory can neither possess religious value nor make theological sense. Error is error and nonsense is nonsense in every realm of thought. Problems there may be in understanding the relation of history to faith, and unresolved paradoxes that attest the finiteness of human understanding; but irreconcilable paradoxes there cannot be if they attest the inconsistency of God or the irrationality of his universe. If God cannot contradict himself, neither can general revelation contradict special revelation, neither can scientific truth contradict biblical truth, and neither can valid philosophical reasoning contradict valid theological reasoning. Just as a careful logic cannot allow contradictory truths without forfeiting the laws of thought, so a consistent theism cannot allow contradictory truths without forfeiting the veracity of God. Rather, when problems arise, the data are incomplete or misunderstood, or else the reasoning processes are fallacious or inconclusive.

God is the ultimate source of all knowledge, and his knowledge provides the ultimate standard of all truth. Augustine insisted on this and argued further that one cannot reason himself out of reason. Truth is one, and a working relationship between Christianity and philosophy can best be developed on this premise. On the contrary, movements such as positivism and existentialism which make a disjunction between fact and value, history and faith, science and religion, or reason and faith, and which thereby relegate Christianity to the extra- or supra-logical, are both self-destructive from the viewpoint of logical consistency and incompatible with historic Christianity.

Our third observation regarding the truth-claims of Christianity is that while the essence of Christian faith is a total and continuing commitment to God in Christ, yet it involves the believer in a commitment to certain objective truths and historical facts understood in clear-cut ways.

Some people think of faith as an emotive response devoid of any rationale. What cannot be understood might be believed. What cannot be demonstrated might be "accepted on faith." This view is both psychologically and biblically inadequate. In the first place, faith must have a known object and beliefs must have cognitive content. For this reason the church has always endeavored to clarify by its preaching and teaching that truth to which response is sought. Faith that is totally devoid of understanding is more like the behavioral response of an animal than genuine belief. Paul said, "I know whom I have believed." In the second place, faith involves a rationale. It is no blind leap in the dark. It gives "a reason for the hope" it prizes. Beginning with its earliest apologists the church has adduced evidences of varied sorts in vindication of its claims. Faith that involves clear ideas and a significant rationale cannot be purely emotive. What then is it?

The Bible makes no disjunction between head and heart. A careful study of the term "heart" in Scripture unfolds its evident meaning: the ruling center of the entire personality. Rational functions are ascribed to the heart more than are emotive functions. To say that a man believes "in his heart," then, asserts that he is committed at the very roots of his life. To be a "wholehearted" believer is to be totally committed. Similarly the biblical picture of faith, given under such metaphors as accepting, following, eating and drinking, suggests complete participation, a life-commitment. Verbal assent alone is not faith; faith must issue in a new texture of life. What is needed is "faith that works by love." Theologians therefore speak of faith as committing the entire person to God, not only his "religious" activities but all of his values and ideas—the rational as well as the emotive aspects of his life.

Faith is a function of the entire personality. Early martyrs died rather than renounce their beliefs, because that would have retracted their total commitment. The early church formulated the Apostles' Creed as a statement of basic truths to be subscribed to by all purported converts. Total Christian faith inevitably commits one to objective truths pertaining to metaphysics *(I believe in God the Father Almighty, Maker of heaven and earth)*, to the miraculous *(born of the Virgin Mary)*, to history *(suffered under Pontius Pilate)*, and to morals *(He shall come to judge the quick and the dead)*.

It is impossible to mistake the intent of the early Christians. Fact and value, objective truth and subjective experience were wholly inseparable within their one total commitment of faith in Jesus Christ. Vital faith and rational contemplation are not antithetical. It is not a case of either/or. To regard the crisis of faith as an uncovering of the inscrutable ground of our being, or an attainment to authentic existence, or a mystical experience unrelated to the historic work of Christ as man's only Savior from sin, is as fallacious as to regard it as simply a mental assent to historical facts or objective truths. Faith integrates both subjective and objective factors. This, in fact, is the genius of genuine Christian faith—that it commits the believer wholeheartedly to One about whose person and work he has gained clear-cut and reasonable convictions. To this the spirited controversies of apostolic, patristic and Reformation days bear abundant witness. Faith is a clearheaded involvement.

Christianity then is not a religion of culturally irrelevant vagaries. It appeals for a faith so complete that it will make possible not only a clear mental formulation of Christian ideas and values, but also a vital experience that remolds both men and culture. Christianity is a religion, not a philosophy; but as a religion it seeks to redeem both the men who do philosophy and the culture that shapes them. It is at the very root of things, and its effect upon philosophy is both inevitable and pervasive. It is a momentous movement that cannot be ignored and must not be underestimated.

CHAPTER 3

Christianity & Philosophy

In the foregoing pages it has been suggested that philosophy as historically seen and practiced pursues two objectives which provide it with a twofold function in human culture. The quest for clear understanding makes philosophy something of an intellectual conscience; the elaboration of a coherent world view from its theoretical bases onwards contributes to the development of other phases of culture. It has been further suggested that Christianity as historically seen and practiced proclaims a message centering in the person and work of Jesus Christ. While it teaches that the intended impact of revelation and redemption is contingent upon the subjective work of God's Spirit in the individual believer, it also affirms certain objective truths and historical facts. These obviously provide a point of contact between Christianity and philosophy. What further can be said as to the relationship between these two enterprises as we have come to understand them?

Variant Attitudes

History reveals a variety of approaches to the question. Each reflects its own milieu and each, we suggest, could be examined in the light of its understanding of Christianity and philosophy respectively. That the relationship we posit between the two depends on our understanding of each is a truism.

An approach which repudiates philosophy as unchristian was epitomized in antiquity by Tertullian of Carthage. Born around 160 A.D., trained as a lawyer, converted to Christianity in his early thirties, he was an ardent and somewhat impetuous apologist. In his reaction against the encroachments of Gnostic rationalism, Tertullian branded philosophy as futile and destructive. "What has Jerusalem to do with Athens?" he asked, and declared, "I believe what is absurd." He was responding to the Gnostic claim that because matter is evil, it is absurd to think a good God would become flesh. He argued that the incarnation is nonetheless reasonable, but his attitude to philosophy is clear. He decried all attempts at a Christian Platonism or Aristotelianism as well as Gnosticism, on the grounds that the man who has found Christ has found the Truth and does not need philosophy. Yet he overlooked his own indebtedness to philosophy in adopting the Stoics' traducian view regarding the origin of the human soul. It is as impossible to detach oneself entirely from philosophical ideas or Christianity entirely from culture as it is to detach faith from life.

Yet subsequent history exhibits individuals with kindred, although perhaps less extreme, tendencies. Repulsed by Descartes' unbounded rationalistic optimism, Blaise Pascal followed Montaigne and the Greek sceptics in reasoning that metaphysical arguments are all equipollent. Such philosophical argumentation is irrelevant to Christianity. The heart has its reasons for believing, but these are intuitive and personal rather than strictly logical. Sören Kierkegaard likewise recoiled from the rationalism of the Enlightenment and from Hegel's relentlessly logical system because they miss the unpredictable and paradoxical character of historical existence. Logical systems, he asserted, are a presumptuous, ineffective and comical substitute for the vitality of life and faith and love. Christianity is characterized more by passionate concern than by the objectivity of an age of reason.

None of these writers actually claims that Christianity is irrational, and it is hard to know what such a claim might mean. If Christian doctrine defies clarification and God lies hidden in the smog of total incomprehensibility, then traditional revelation-claims are denied. If biblical assertions are contrary to fact or self-contradictory, then the rationality of God is reduced to a sheer equivocation. It seems therefore that what this repudiation of philosophy really amounts to is a rejection more of certain types of philosophy than of reason in any and every form. Problems arise more in relating Christianity to certain kinds of rationalism or irrationalism, and in squaring its doctrines with the particular teachings of particular philosophers, than in relating the faith in principle to philosophical inquiry.

A second traditional approach to our problem is one which compromises the claims not of philosophy but of Christianity. The Christian Gnostics of patristic times provide classic examples. So desirous were they of integrating Christianity into prevalent thought-patterns that they forfeited the distinctives of the faith. Some of the early apologists who successfully resisted Gnosticism exaggerated the similarities of Christianity to other philosophies. Justin Martyr, for instance, virtually identifying John's *Logos* with those of Plato and the Stoics, inferred that all who live according to reason are Christians, Socrates and others included.

Similar cases could be cited from modern times. Descartes was a Christian theist. But his rationalistic separation of philosophy from theology, and his addition of a mechanistic view of nature, led others to view supernatural revelation and redemption as unnecessary. Enlightenment deism resulted. Nineteenth-century liberal theology developed in similar style. Immanuel Kant reduced Christianity to a symbolic expression of man's sense of moral duty, and Friedrich Schleiermacher gave it a Romanticist twist by interpreting Christian doctrine as a projection of man's feelings of one-ness with nature and dependence on Being-itself. Likewise with existential theology: Paul Tillich provides a good example. Theology, he claims, answers the existential questions which philosophy uncovers. But the questions he uncovers are limited by his phenomenological method to questions of existential ontology, so that his theology loses much of the distinctive content of Christian revelation and redemption. Tillich's God is no longer a transcendent personal agent whose saving acts bring hope into the world.

A third traditional approach tries to relate faith to reason and Christianity to philosophy without compromising the values of either. Two historical examples provide the landmarks. Augustine of Hippo, combatting the Manichean rationalism from which he had been converted, recognized the indispensable contributions of the Christian revelation to his understanding. He also found a valuable ally in the Neoplatonism to which Bishop Ambrose had introduced him. Insisting that reason is a divine gift, he brought philosophy to the fight against sceptics and rationalists alike. Insisting that Christianity is a divine revelation, he presented it as the sure answer to man's intellectual and moral woes. Faith and reason, for him, are inseparably intertwined: Each step of conscious faith inevitably involves some reasoning; and each process of reasoning consciously or unconsciously involves some act of faith. "Faith is understanding's step and understanding is faith's reward." Augustine's work shaped early Medieval thought, influenced the Franciscans and Calvin and present-day Reformed traditions.

Thomas Aquinas developed the most widespread synthesis among Roman Catholic thinkers, one frequently followed by non-Reformed Protestants. So impressed was he by Aristotle's valuable contributions that Thomas came to regard the Christian revelation more as supplementing than as correcting and transforming Greek philosophical insights. Natural philosophy can demonstrate the premises of revealed theology: the existence of God and the immortality of the soul. But grace alone can introduce us to what lies beyond this line, where reason's task becomes one of explicating and systematizing revealed truths.

Contemporary evangelicals vary on the subject. At the one extreme, some popular voices express a Tertullian-like position, others an Augustinian or Thomistic or Cartesian position, or some new position generated by existential or analytic thought. Some of these views are represented in the bibliography at the end of this booklet. Any detailed proposal would represent the writer's own interpretation of a given tradition and that is not the present purpose. Rather we shall set up some guideposts to enable the reader to explore further the basic problem involved.

The Basic Problem

Undergirding all questions concerning the relation of Christianity to philosophy lies the obvious fact that the Christian religion lives in a pagan culture and the obvious implication that it must without compromise adapt itself to the task of living in and communicating with that culture. If Christians are to understand, appreciate and profit from their faith, they must be able to think about it in ways that they themselves find meaningful—ways shaped by their culture with its traditions, education, language and philosophies. If Christians are to understand their history and culture, and even the history of theology, they must understand the philosophies that shape these things. If Christians are to communicate their faith to others it must be in ways that are meaningful to others, ways provided by the culture they share: traditions, education, language, philosophies, etc. The history of philosophy and of Christian theology and of apologetics, and the transforming effect of the gospel on the intellectual life of the individual and the culture, attest this inevitable interaction.

Biblical Examples

The first guidepost to such understanding is provided by New Testament examples of the relationship between Christianity and philosophy. The apostles both faced the problems and used the opportunities presented by the philosophies of their day. Three passages assume major significance: 1 Corinthians 1—2, Colossians and John 1.

In 1 Corinthians Paul makes a distinction between the wisdom of the world and that of God. He asserts that the latter, not the former, leads man to the knowledge of God; that whereas the world scoffs at the revealed wisdom of God, the world's wisdom is really foolish by comparison. It should be observed first that Paul is writing of his initial visit to Corinth following his experience with the Athenian philosophers (Acts 17). The Epicureans and Stoics of Athens were both materialists, and even the Platonists would undoubtedly have joined in ridiculing the notion of a resurrection. To the Greek mind it was both undesirable and impossible. They preferred their rationalistic conclusions to the message of the Cross. In explaining this to the Corinthians, Paul points out that biases so deeply rooted in the thought-patterns of a culture ("the world") are not likely to be dispelled by counter-assertions alone, no matter how powerfully argued. Only the power of God can confound them; only the Spirit of God can instruct them effectively. *He* makes objective truth subjectively acceptable.

In the Colossian epistle Paul is combatting a heresy akin to later forms of Gnosticism. Rooted in a rationalistic epistemology, it presented a metaphysic that made Christ one of a series of emanations from God, and it taught a rigid asceticism as the way of salvation from an evil, material world. In reply the apostle postulates certain essentials of a Christian world view. He argues that Jesus Christ is the focus of all wisdom; he who knows Christ has learned the mystery that gives perspective to other truth. Christ is the eternal Creator of the cosmos; he who knows Christ has gained overall direction for his metaphysic. Christ is the crucified and risen Redeemer; he who knows Christ has found deliverance from the evil lurking in his own soul; he lives and works within the institutions

CHRISTIANITY AND PHILOSOPHY

of his society, motivated by devotion to Christ and guided by the moral teaching of Christ and his apostles.

It should be observed that while Paul warns against a philosophy rooted exclusively in the principles and traditions of human culture, he nevertheless recognizes the possibility of philosophy being "after Christ" (Col. 2:8). Nor does he divorce his own Christian philosophizing from its cultural setting; rather, he employs the terminology of the very movement to which he objects—terms such as "wisdom," "knowledge," "fullness," "mystery" and "philosophy" itself. Did he use such terminology with none of its original meaning, he would merely equivocate; the Gnostics would use a given term in sense A and he would use it in sense B; the two senses would have nothing in common; the word itself would convey nothing. Did he use their terminology uncritically and make predications akin to their own, then he and they would differ not at all. But by the skillful use of words in new contexts, he successfully modified their meanings while drawing sufficiently close analogies to make the necessary contact with cultural thought-patterns.

In the first chapter of his Gospel, John uses the philosophical term *Logos* to describe Jesus Christ. Heraclitus had used it to refer to the order apparent in a world of change. The Stoics followed his example, rooting such order in an impersonal though rational cosmic force, a *Logos* that operated through its multiplied *logoi spermatikoi*. Philo, the Alexandrian Jew, identified this *Logos* with the *wisdom* of Hebrew literature, but certainly failed to regard it as a coequal person in an eternal Divine Trinity. John makes use of the same term. Undoubtedly he is dependent on the Old Testament conception of the spoken word of God as a creative act (Gen. 1:3) and on the Hebrew personification of divine wisdom (Prov. 8). But he neither empties the Greek term of all its own meaning nor uses it simply in any one of its previous meanings. He speaks of the *Logos* as both identical with God and distinguishable within the

Godhead. He speaks of him as the Personal Creator, the source of both being and order. He asserts that this *Logos* became incarnate to reveal the Father and redeem men. This is another case of the adaptation of language and concepts as a means of orienting the Christian message in a pagan environment, a means employed ever since, whether in the trinitarian formulations of the church fathers, the scholastic doctrine of analogy or contemporary discussions of religious language. Similar conclusions could be drawn from the treatment in 1 John of yet another variety of Gnosticism.

From these biblical examples, then, we elicit the following principles:

1. In the final analysis the minds of men molded by pagan thought-patterns are won, not by philosophical argument or rhetorical device, but by the power of God's Word and the work of the Holy Spirit.

2. Since a pagan philosophy can distort one's understanding of reality and of life, a Christian philosophy becomes necessary in order to work out clearly and systematically the philosophical implications of the Christian revelation.

3. One means available to the Christian thinker is the analogy that exists between Christian beliefs and ideas current in the culture. This involves using the philosophical concepts and methods and language of the day. But whereas the rationalist and liberal traditions modified Christian concepts and adapted them to cultural uses, the biblical writers modified cultural concepts and adapted them to Christian use.

Common Ground
The use of current philosophical tools, whether to clarify the Christian's own understanding or to communicate an understanding of the faith to others, requires that we identify the common ground between believers and unbelievers which makes communication possible. Such common ground is of two kinds: the generic, which is common to all men, and the cultural, which is common within a

CHRISTIANITY AND PHILOSOPHY

given culture. Generic likenesses are rooted in the fact that all men are created in the image of God. In that all are rational creatures, they have in common an obligation to the basic laws of thought; no man can equivocate or contradict himself while thinking properly. In that all are moral creatures, they have in common an obligation to moral law. Whether or not they recognize the law of God, there persists some sense of "oughtness" related to basic areas of value which all men share—areas such as the family, property, physical well-being—in the context of which different cultures formulate their moral codes. In that all are similarly constituted psychologically, all men have in common certain basic needs, the satisfaction of which is one of life's greatest demands. Undoubtedly the rational, moral and psychological are all closely interrelated, and further categories could probably be added. But the generic similarities found in such traits as these provide a common basis that facilitates the Christian use of the philosophical stock in trade of the non-Christian world.

Christian theology asserts that the image of God in man is distorted by sin. In so far as this affects non-Christian understandings, moral sensitivity and psychological needs—to use the examples selected above—the common ground is disturbed. Indeed, the religious root from which thought and life grow is different in the unbeliever than in the believer. It should be noted, however, that while human depravity extends into all areas of the personality, it does not totally destroy normative human traits. Wrong priorities, sinful attitudes, godless motivation indeed corrupt them. A man's thinking will accordingly be distorted, and more so in closer proximity to the crucial issue of the knowledge of God in Christ. But he can never escape his obligation to the laws of thought or to the evidence in the case; nonsense is still nonsense and error is still error. Moreover, his moral sensitivity may be dulled and his moral code distorted, but he remains a moral being with recognized obligations. He may repress his basic psychological needs or seek satisfaction for them in perverse ways that build in him a grossly distorted personality, but the needs persistently exhibit themselves in life's frustrations, tensions and psychoses. In other words, regardless of all the distortion of the image of God, a man remains a man. God does not allow his creation to be corrupted beyond measure. He preserves sufficient common ground to make possible both understanding and communication.

Cultural likenesses exist among members of the same culture. Western culture, in the Greco-Roman tradition as affected by the Hebrew-Christian religions, provides common ground for mutual understanding and communication. Oriental cultures provide the same. Within common cultures communication and understanding are easier than between different cultures. To the extent, then, that Christians are members of a given culture they are thereby enabled to use the tools of that culture in orienting Christianity to prevailing thought-patterns. Here is common ground.

There is a sense in which the Christian does not fit his culture. His ideas and values, being biblically based, are often at variance with those of unredeemed men and an unredeemed culture. This, however, does not gainsay the obvious, that he is still compelled to make use of the tools of his culture in explicating and expressing his faith. After all, he has no tools other than these.

The Primacy of Revelation

The apostolic use of current philosophical tools is to be distinguished from that of the rationalist or of many modern theologians. Whereas the latter tend to conform Christian ideas to the cultural, the apostles sought to adapt the cultural to the Christian. It is here that historic orthodoxy parts company with modern liberalism and existential theology. The liberal is willing to dispense with biblical concepts—whether of revelation or of the Trinity or of the atonement—in order to make his message acceptable in his culture. Tillich and Bultmann radically alter biblical concepts in adapting to the existential mood. The conservative, on the other hand, insists with Augustine and the Reformers on the primacy of revelation; the Scriptures are his final and sufficient rule of both faith and practice. If current concepts and moods differ from the biblical, then they are at fault and must be corrected. If they are analogous to the biblical, then they may be carefully employed in the explication of Christian thought.

This may readily be illustrated. Take the Marxist view of history. Its economic determinism claims that all phases of human life are and always have been governed by the economic forces that produce class warfare. The Christian philosopher disagrees. While he cannot deny that economic forces have played a significant part in history, and especially since the Industrial Revolution, yet from an objective viewpoint he sees history as an extremely complex process. To single out economic causes above all others is an oversimplification; the "proof" offered by Marx and Lenin suffers from incomplete induction and amounts to a hasty generalization. Our philosopher finds man's rational, moral and spiritual characteristics hard to account for within the limits of a Marxist behaviorism. He finds in Christianity's doctrine of the image of God and its distortion by sin a preferable perspective from which to understand both the uniqueness of man and the regrettable class struggle. As a Christian, moreover, he has come to regard the complexities of history as somehow reflecting the providential activity of his God. From starting points such as these he approaches the philosophy of history with its concomitant problems in ethics and metaphysics.

But beyond a certain point his commitment to the primacy of revelation does not lead him as clearly. Christianity indeed claims to meet the basic needs of men. But this does not mean that every intellectual perplexity is *ipso facto* dispelled. The precise philosophical expression of the nature of man, the relationship of mind to matter, the extent of environmental influence on human behavior, the degree of objectivity available in historical knowledge, the choice between divergent views of the a priori—in these and other questions the decision of the Christian philosopher becomes as much or even more a matter of philosophical preference as of religious commitment. He could hardly be a complete materialist, it is true, but he could conceivably be either an idealist or a dualist. He could hardly be a deist but might follow either Aquinas or Kant in the value ascribed to the theistic arguments. He may come to regard a particular view of historical knowledge or of the theistic arguments as more useful to the Christian apologist than some other view, or even as more consistent with his particular tradition within the Christian religion; but in these debatable matters his commitment is made more on philosophic than on biblical grounds.

Christianity gives considerable direction and motivation to philosophy. But it is not a philosophy, nor does its revelation lead unequivocally to the sort of closed and dogmatic system which modern existentialism and analysis despise. One cannot infer from Christian premises conclusive answers to every philosophical problem. It is for this reason that even Christian philosophers differ. Their philosophies, like those of their non-Christian colleagues, reflect a variety of influences and viewpoints. They, too, are engaged in the quest for a degree of clarity and a kind of system that may for the present remain elusive.

The Christian Philosopher

What, then, is the function of the Christian in philosophy? A threefold answer is possible. First, the Christian philosopher may serve theology. Sir William Hamilton once asserted that "no difficulty emerges in theology which has not previously emerged in philosophy." If this is so, the Christian philosopher will contribute to the discussion of theological problems old and new a penetrating insight, which will help him not only to distinguish truth from error but also to understand the truth in terms that are meaningful to the contemporary mind. He will avoid the obscurity of hackneyed clichés and of terms now ambiguous or passé; and, as was done in historical discussions of the Trinity, the origin of the human soul, and so forth, he will bring to the work of systematization the tools of philosophy.

The Christian philosopher may also serve apologetics; in doing so he will speak not to the church, as he does in theology, but to the world. He will strive for a clarity of understanding, a consistency of argument and a contemporaneity of expression which, by humble dependence on the illuminating power of the Holy Spirit, will commend the faith to the secular mind. He will seek to show that Christianity is intellectually respectable, that it is relevant, that it is defensible, that it is the most appealing of all the voices which clamor for the ears of contemporary man.

Finally, the Christian philosopher may serve his culture. Here he does what any philosopher does, but he does it as a Christian. The philosopher, we have observed, serves two functions: By his quest for clarity he serves as an intellectual conscience; by developing a coherent world view he serves as a cultural guide. The Christian philosopher, benefiting from the light of revelation and seeking clarity of understanding on the same philosophical problems as his non-Christian colleague, provides a Christian intellectual conscience for his age. He will, perhaps, be most concerned about confusions and inconsistencies in areas that bear directly on the faith: Philosophy of religion, philosophy of mind, ethics and social philosophy especially are likely to appeal, but not exclusively. For his concern for truth and clarity in any area of thought bears witness to the concern of the Christian faith and life for every perplexity of the human mind.

The Christian philosopher, moreover, will want to develop as far as he can a Christian world-and-life view—one which sees life steadily, as a whole and from the perspective of biblical revelation. His epistemology will take into account the place of faith and revelation; his metaphysics will be guided by his theism with its doctrine of creation; his ethics will embrace the law of God and Christ's redemption; his philosophy of history will see the world process as moving under the providence of the Judge of all men. But he will not confine himself to translating theology into philosophical language. Rather he will try to incorporate these Christian ideas and values that are also discussed in theology into the broader scope of a system that respects also materials and problems which are common to a given culture or to men generically. From this perspective he may speak to his day, seeking as do other philosophers to shed light on the varied problems and changing structures of human experience. He will stand as a responsible member of society, sensitive in soul and alert to the bewildering conflicts of an onrushing history. He will come not to be ministered unto but to minister.

J. V. L. Casserley expresses it succinctly in his work *The Christian in Philosophy:* "... this is the high prophetic office of a Christian philosopher, but it is one that can only be fulfilled by a Christian philosophy so rigorously philosophical that the most obstinately 'pure' philosopher will admit it to his discussions, and at the same time so manifestly a way of grace that the simplest and most unphilosophical Christian will remember it in his prayers."[1]

CHAPTER 4

Christians
In Philosophy

Some philosophers are Christians, and some Christians are philosophers. But Christianity is not itself a philosophy, and from what we have said it can be seen that there is no one Christian philosophy in the sense of one uniform and necessary position on every philosophical question. Rather philosophy in any tradition, Christian or naturalistic or whatever, is an exploratory activity with changing foci and methods; and it is pluralistic, for it produces a variety of possible positions on many topics rather than one monolithic stance.

To appreciate this variety among Christians in philosophy, we have to understand some of the variables involved. One which emerges from the brief account given earlier of the nature of philosophy is a matter of style: Some philosophers operate more analytically than systematically, while some are more systematic than analytic. The reason for this is partly historical, so that contemporary English-speaking philosophy generally has a more analytic style than it did a hundred years ago. But it is also partly a matter of temperament: Some personalities are more disposed towards what

George Berkeley called "minute philosophy" than to "philosophy in the grand style" that elaborates a world view.

There are also more technical reasons for variety historically among Christians in philosophy, as there are for philosophical variety generally: A particular problem receives concerted attention for a while or a new method develops. The last few years, for example, have seen the focus move from problems about religious language to classic problems of philosophical theology, from meta-ethical discussion to problems in social ethics, from the positivist's demand for empirical verifiability to the study of speech acts and the relation of knowledge to belief. As philosophical interests and methods change, so the activity of Christians in philosophy is likely too to change.

Cultural changes also bring new philosophical emphases. This was true of Socrates' work in ancient Athens; it was true in the Renaissance and Enlightenment, true of the optimism of the nineteenth century and of the more gloomy mid-twentieth century. And the activism of the 1960s generated new philosophical interest in problems of social philosophy, ranging from alienation and war to abortion and women's rights.

In this chapter, however, we want to concentrate on just two factors, one of which gives continuity to Christian thought and the other of which produces differences. The first we shall call "perspective" and the second "models."

Christian Perspective

History exhibits several major perspectival traditions that persist from antiquity to the present, each of which is united around the basic beliefs of a particular world view. A naturalistic tradition is discernible from the pre-Socratics to the Stoics and Epicureans to Hobbes (with qualifications) and to Russell and Dewey and contemporary philosophical naturalists. For all the differences within it, this tradition is united in the attempt to explain everything by reference to the physical, whether mind and value, or religion and art, or whatever. We may also trace an idealist tradition from Plato to Plotinus and the Christian Platonists, to Berkeley and Hegel and Bradley and Royce. For all their differences, they unite in the belief that some immaterial reality underlies every experience we have. Somewhat overlapping with the idealists is a theistic tradition that runs from Clement of Alexandria to Augustine and Aquinas to Descartes and Berkeley, to A. E. Taylor and E. S. Brightman and analysts like Ian Ramsey or Alvin Plantinga. I have listed only Christian representatives, but one might also list Jewish and Moslem philosophers, for all three theistic religions have contributed.

Christian philosophy is thus "perspectival": It is part of a theistic tradition in the history of thought. For all its many varieties, it is united around the basic beliefs that comprise a distinctively Christian perspective in philosophy. And so we must pause to ask what those beliefs are.

The question is a little different from that of chapter two, where our concern was with the distinctives of Christianity among the religions of the world. Now our concern is with the *philosophical* distinctives of a Christian perspective. Basically they are two: the relation of God and creation, and the condition of man in sin and grace. The first involves the doctrines of creation *ex nihilo* and *ad extra*, and implies the contingency of all created things. It affects the problem of freedom and necessity, the nature of God and evil, the values of art and of social institutions and the basis of meaning in life. The second involves the doctrine of the image of God in man and affects the possibility of man's achieving freedom, knowing and achieving the good, and realizing meaning in life.

These two distinctives of a Christian perspective have a bearing on epistemological problems and on metaphysical problems, as well as on ethics and aesthetics, political and legal philosophy, the philosophy of history and so forth. Exactly *how* that bearing is worked out depends on other factors involved in doing philosophy, as well as on the perspective itself. But the Christian mind at work in philosophy is properly characterized by an awareness of these two germinal factors.[2] The first distinguishes Christian philosophy from non-theistic traditions, and the second distinguishes it from non-Christian varieties of theism.

Philosophical Models

The basic perspective is what Christians in philosophy have in common. One thing they do not have in common is their use of *models*, the same models, in fact, as are used by philosophers in other perspectival traditions.

To illustrate this and at the risk of over-simplification, let us consider briefly three historical models drawn from science. While models are also evident in the history of art and literature and of our social institutions, we shall concentrate simply on their influence in philosophy, particularly among Christians.[3]

The Greek model developed gradually out of the attempts of earlier Greek philosophy and science to explain order and unity amid the change and diversity of nature. It was systematized by Aristotle in a way that shaped Western thought and art right up through the Medieval era. Aristotelian science, first of all, accounted for the order of nature and the similarities of things by a system of classification that included genera and species. It explained the unchanging unity of a species by the theory of forms, so that a particular thing is composed of matter and form, the latter being an unchanging principle that defines what the thing can become. It gives to the thing the essential nature of its species. Second, Aristotelian science explained all kinds of change by reference to the same four kinds of causes: material (like the marble of which a statue is made), formal (the form of the species, the ideal represented by the statue), efficient (the agent doing the work, the sculptor's chiselling) and final (the end or purpose for which a change occurs, e.g., to adorn the Parthenon).

This Greek model dominated Western thought for some seventeen hundred years, and in philosophy it captured the imagination of Christian as well as non-Christian thinkers. Augustine employed a neo-Platonic version of it in discussing how God ordered his creation and how we may understand both good and evil. Aquinas employed a more purely Aristotelian version in discussing nature, man and God. Thus nature is ordered by unchanging forms which are known eternally to God but are immanent in the creation and give to it a pattern of fixed species and genera replete with natural ends to which all things move. A man's rational soul is the form of his species, individuated by association with his particular body but animating that body and ruling his life. From this view arises a natural law ethic, for the natural ends which we seek, such as self-preservation, sexual reproduction, social relationships for the common good, and a knowledge of God, are good by virtue of the very nature of things. Even Thomas' famous five proofs for the existence of God start with Aristotelian premises about an order of efficient causes and formal and final causes. In brief, his entire philosophy is shaped by the Greek model he adopted.

Some critics have argued that this makes his system Greek rather than Christian. My suggestion, rather, is that the Christian core of it is clearly there, in his view of God and creation, and of man in sin and grace—even though Reformed theologians may formulate those doctrines somewhat differently—and that he has converted the Greek model to the service of his Christian perspective. By doing so he was able to address, as Christians in philosophy should, not only the philosophical problems of the day but also the apologetic and theological issues faced by the church.

Some were dissatisfied with Aquinas then, and others still are. With his view of faith and reason, he makes philosophy too autonomous for the Augustinian; and his theory of forms is said to deprive God of his freedom by subordinating the divine will to the unchanging necessities of eternal forms. Finally, men like William of Occam rejected the Greek model altogether, on both philosophical and theological grounds.

The Renaissance model developed from the mechanistic science of that period and was systematized by Isaac Newton. Here the Greek forms are rejected and any consideration of purpose in nature is left for theologians to discuss. Rather, order is explained by the operation of fixed laws of motion on the particles of matter that comprise our physical world. It is a "billiard ball universe," regular and predictable in its actions, subject to principles like inertia and gravitation.

Descartes adopted this model long before Newton. His account of the human body and the material world depends directly on the mechanics of his day, and his discussion of the operations of the mind is built on the same analogy: Ideas are particles of consciousness moved and conjoined by laws of thought. God is the first cause not only of the whole chain of physical motions but also of undeniable ideas that move intuitively within the mind. Others extended the model to language and to society. Language is composed of its own particles of matter (words) and laws of motion (rules of syntax, and of logic), and society is likewise composed of isolated individuals impelled by their individual rights into the social contracts that structure our domestic and political institutions. The rule of laws in society is analogous to the rule of natural forces in the material world.

But again not everyone was satisfied. It seemed to some, like Berkeley, Samuel Clarke and Leibniz—all of them earnest Christians—that the mechanistic model left God as a remote cause rather than an immanent creator. The deists, in fact, drew that conclusion and rejected such acts of God as special revelation, miracles and the incarnation. To counter these tendencies in the mechanistic view, Berkeley denied the independent reality of matter and physical forces, and argued for a world composed entirely of minds and their ideas, for then our involuntary physical experiences must be caused by a mind, the Supreme Mind in fact, rather than by matter in action. Samuel Clarke, a close friend of Newton's, for his part suggested that instead of regarding God as an extra-spatial first cause, we should regard space as the "Divine Sensorium," so that everything exists and occurs "in him." Rightly or wrongly, Leibniz accused Clarke of pantheism. He rejected the mechanistic account as too superficial, and in his theory of monads fashioned a novel version of the Greek model instead. The activity of these Christians in philosophy can be understood in terms of this interplay of perspective and models.

For various reasons the nineteenth century rejected the mechanistic model. In science, developmental biology was emerging, both in genetics and in evolutionary theory, to replace earlier vitalistic and mechanistic views. In physics, electromagnetic field theory and, later, quantum mechanics and relativity theory cut the empirical ground from beneath Newtonian physics. *A more dynamic or organismic model* began to emerge, in the arts as romanticism and in philosophy as "process-metaphysics."

One major example is the German philosopher Hegel, the famous idealist who traced the historical evolution of consciousness, then of reason and culture, through a dialectical process of thesis, antithesis and synthesis. The conflict of opposites in this process generates new levels of emergence from more primitive manifestations of the underlying spiritual reality of things.

Contrary to some popular interpretations, Hegel does not reject traditional laws of logic such as the principle of non-contradiction. He explicitly affirms those laws, but claims that they are trivial when applied to organic processes and historical change, for organic changes both negate the original constituents and preserve them in new ways, and in the course of history nothing altogether escapes change. The dialectic, then, is a logic of history and of change, while the traditional laws of logic are the rules that govern the unchanging identity of eternal forms. Perhaps Hegel unduly separates the two, but his major contribution remains: He developed a new process model to replace both the fixed forms of Aristotle and the fixed laws of motion of the mechanists.

Hegel had Christian roots, but the religious consequences of his philosophy contributed more to the rise of liberal theology than either to orthodox theology or to philosophy from the Christian perspective we outlined above. In reaction against its misinterpretation by deists using the mechanistic model, he explicitly rejects the doctrine of *ex nihilo* creation, and develops instead a more organic conception of God's immanence in the creation. As an idealist he holds that everything is a manifestation of the one spiritual reality that underlies everything. That reality is Absolute Spirit, which religious language calls God. Everything in existence, therefore, is a manifestation of the underlying Divine Being: Both the evolutionary process and the unfolding consciousness of the human spirit are God's self-revelation, a revelation that comes to its fullest expression not in science as the deists implied, nor in art as the Romanticists held, nor even in religion, but in philosophy. Artistic representations and religious symbols are indirect anticipations of the rational concepts of philosophy.

Hegel's conception of man in sin and grace suffers similarly. The individual human spirit, which is God's image in man, is but a passing moment in the unfolding manifestation of Absolute Spirit, rather than a finite being created out of nothing to image God in its own free and responsible acts. Hegel therefore had problems with freedom and responsibility and he fathered subsequent collectivist and totalitarian political ideologies. Moreover, the fall of man into sin is no longer for him a historical fact but a myth which points to the non-rational and non-spiritual condition from which the human spirit is emerging. Jesus Christ is no longer the eternal Creator who acts for our redemption by incarnating himself in history, but rather the incarnation story symbolizes the ideal possibilities for man as an evolving embodiment of the Divine Spirit in the world.

Parallel notions arose in Friedrich Schleiermacher and classic liberal theology, and later, with significant modifications due to Whitehead's influence, in the process theology of Charles Hartshorne and others. In these thinkers, the process model drowns out the two basic elements of a Christian perspective in philosophy. Other writers, like William Temple, the former Archbishop of Canterbury, have employed much the same model without such forfeiture, but their influence is now insignificant in comparison with that of the process theologians.

New Directions

The interaction of perspective and model continues. Since Kant emphasized the central role of practical reason in human thought, a personalistic model has gradually been developing. It bears the imprint of thinkers like William James and Sören Kierkegaard, as well as of idealists like E. S. Brightman, and it takes shape in the writings of an American like Peter Bertocci, a Frenchman like Gabriel Marcel and a Scotsman like John Macmurray.[4] Parallel developments appear in recent analytic work on human action. The model which seems to be emerging is drawn from the humanities rather than the natural sciences, for it is in art, literature, ethics and religion that we uncover distinctively human dimensions of existence that are lacking elsewhere in nature.

Human existence is not, as the Romanticists conceived it, a beautifully feelingful experience of oneness with nature. It is indeed rooted in the process of nature, but it is marked by action that transcends the process. The human person is not just a product of forces beyond his control that shape his destiny, but a created creator, an agent who devises new possibilities and helps to shape his own future in directions that nature alone could not. For this reason, models drawn from natural science are inadequate in explaining the human person: They cannot account for our self-transcendence in artistic imagination, moral resolve and creative action. This should not surprise the Christian who believes he is made in the image of a God whose acts transcend the limitations of nature's process.

Present-day philosophical horizons hold alluring possibilities for Christian thought. Perhaps the most crucial areas of current interest relate to the nature of man (the philosophy of mind, of human action and of belief) and to ethics and social philosophy. But the challenge that faces the Christian in philosophy can best be seen in the light of the past. He must scrutinize accepted conceptual models, their presuppositions and their implications, and develop one which can bring Christian perspectives to bear constructively in current philosophical discussion. He can thereby contribute both to apologetics and to theology and culture generally, for the models we have noted in philosophy have been at work there too. But he will need rigorous preparation, a broad grasp of the history of thought, disciplined work, and a mind devoted to the service of God in our day.

NOTES

[1]J. V. L. Casserley, *The Christian in Philosophy* (Charles Scribner's Sons, 1951), p. 262.
[2]These two considerations are expounded more fully in the "Christian Philosophy" article in the 15th edition of *Encyclopaedia Britannica* (1974) and in other materials listed in the bibliography.
[3]See Floyd Matson, *The Broken Image* (Doubleday, 1964).
[4]See especially Macmurray's *The Self as Agent* (Faber and Faber, 1969) and Robert Blaikie's theological application of this model in *Secular Christianity and the God Who Acts* (Eerdmans, 1970).

SUGGESTED FURTHER READING

The following list, though somewhat arbitrary, is intended to represent significant contributions to an understanding of the problem as a whole.

Brown, Colin. *Philosophy and the Christian Faith.* InterVarsity Press, 1969. A brief but highly readable history of the relation of philosophy to theology since Aquinas.

Casserley, J. V. L. *The Christian in Philosophy.* Charles Scribner's Sons, 1951. An historical approach to the contemporary problem of subjectivity and objectivity, focusing on the function of Christian philosophers.

Dooyeweerd, H. *In the Twilight of Western Thought.* Presbyterian and Reformed Publishing Co., 1960. An influential Dutch thinker's American lectures about the radically Christian root of theoretical thought.

Geisler, Norman. *Philosophy of Religion.* Zondervan, 1974. A recent textbook by an evangelical with reasoned conclusions.

Gilkey, J. Langdon. *Maker of Heaven and Earth.* Doubleday, 1959. A lucid discussion of the meaning and implications of creation *ex nihilo*.

Gill, Jerry. *The Possibility of Religious Knowledge.* Eerdmans, 1971. A creative and up-to-date treatment of our knowledge of God.

Gilson, Etienne. *Reason and Revelation in the Middle Ages.* Charles Scribner's Sons, 1938. A contemporary Thomistic scholar lucidly traces the problem from its inception in patristic times. An introductory treatment which brings the medieval positions into focus.

Holmes, A. F. "Christian Philosophy," *Encyclopaedia Britannica.* 15th edition, 1974.

———. *Christian Philosophy in the Twentieth Century.* Craig Press, 1969. A study of philosophical methodology and the idea of Christian philosophy.

———. *Faith Seeks Understanding.* Eerdmans, 1971. An examination of current theories of scientific, historical, moral, personal and religious knowledge.

Mavrodes, George. *Belief in God.* Random House, 1970. A brief analysis of the case for and problems with theistic belief.

Miller, Ed L. *God and Reason*. Macmillan, 1972. An historically oriented introduction to borderland problems between philosophy and theology.

Nédoncelle, M. *Is There a Christian Philosophy?* Hawthorn Books, 1960. A good introduction to a crucial question hotly debated since the 1930s.

Niebuhr, Reinhold. *The Nature and Destiny of Man*, Vol. 1. Scribner's 1964. Chapters 1-4 offer a superb critique of non-Christian views of man.

Niebuhr, H. Richard. *Christ and Culture*. Harper & Brothers, 1951. A brilliant discussion of a broader issue, focusing on five viewpoints: radical, accommodationist, synthesist, dualist and conversionist.

Ramsey, Ian. *Models and Mystery*. Oxford, 1964. A succinct discussion of the explanatory role of models in science and theology.

Reid, J. K. S. *Christian Apologetics*. Eerdmans, 1970. An historical overview.

Tresmontant, Claude. *The Origins of Christian Philosophy*. Hawthorn Books, 1963. A brief exposition of major themes in early Christian thought.